ANTHRACITE
ANTRACITE

Bartolo Cattafi

ANTHRACITE
ANTRACITE

Translated by Brian Cole

❧

Introduced by Peter Dale

Arc
PUBLICATIONS
2000

Published by Arc Publications
Nanholme Mill, Shaw Wood Road
Todmorden, Lancs. OL14 6DA

Design Tony Ward
Printed by Arc & Throstle Press
Nanholme Mill, Todmorden Lancs.

ISBN 1 900072 42 4

The Publishers acknowledge financial
assistance from the
Arts Council of England

Arc Publications Visible Poets Series
Editor: Jean Boase-Beier

CONTENTS

Translator's preface / 9
Introduction / 15

SERIES EDITOR'S NOTE

There is a prevailing view of translated poetry, especially in England, which maintains that it should read as though it had originally been written in English. The books in the *Visible Poets* series aim to challenge that view. They assume that the reader of poetry is by definition someone who wants to experience the strange, the unusual, the new, the foreign, someone who delights in the stretching and distortion of language which makes any poetry, translated or not, alive and distinctive. The translators of the poets in this series aim not to hide but to reveal the original, to make it visible and, in so doing, to render visible the translator's task, too. The reader is invited not only to experience the unique fusion of the creative talents of poet and translator embodied in the English poems in these collections, but also to speculate on the processes of their creation and so to gain a deeper understanding and enjoyment of both original and translated poems.

Jean Boase-Beier

Cattafi was a poet who flourished in the very lively post-war Italian cultural scene, but who has not been much translated into English. This selection is an attempt to remedy this situation.

He was born in Barcellona, near Messina in Sicily, in 1922. Inevitably he had to serve in the war, and he was perhaps fortunate to have been taken prisoner and held in the Shetlands. After the war he graduated in law and settled in Milan, where he worked in industry, publishing and journalism. He travelled extensively in Europe and Africa, and his travels were paralleled by a spiritual odyssey, continually seeking some sense in life. In 1967 he returned to his roots in Sicily, where he remained until his death from cancer in March 1979.

Poetry was a spare time activity during his career, but he was very prolific and successful – he was awarded the prestigious literary prize, the Premio Cittadella, in 1959. There is an unexplained gap from January 1963 to February 1971 when he seems to have written nothing, and in 1974 and 1975 he wrote no new poetry, but spent a lot of time editing his papers. After his death a considerable quantity of work, largely unpublished, was collated in collaboration with his wife, Ada, by Giovanni Raboni, and a collection of over 300 poems was published in 1990.

Although Cattafi was a Sicilian, he was regarded in the '50s as one of three poets called the linea lombarda – the others being Luciano Erba and Nelo Risi. This group were part of the "Hermetic Revival" which was concerned to maintain continuity with the poetry of the hermetic tradition, in which, according to the critic Anceschi, "objects (were) intensified and charged to such an extent as to turn the language into a symbol with some references to reality and familiar situations". According to the poet Alan Marshfield "'hermetic' came to refer to ancient lore, especially alchemy, and also to anything sealed, mysterious, cryptic. So the purified image was also a code to be deciphered." These poets were published especially in the magazine Esperienza poetica which stressed the traditional line of poetry. Ideology was rejected, and they aimed to link the new poets with traditional trends by a revision of poetic and cultural values.

What are the problems of translating a poet like Cattafi into English, and what satisfaction is derived from the results? Translators have different views and different satisfactions. Some regard the original as a starting-point and create a new poem on that base – and can often create several versions of the same poem. The

9

present collection is not of that nature: it aims to translate, to convey to the non-Italian speaker the feeling, the essence, of the original. The first essential in this endeavour is to achieve an accurate translation of the meaning of the poems – I am indebted to Gabrina Pounds for her very able help in ensuring this. There is no way that a translator can make a non-Italian-speaking English reader understand the poems as an Italian would, since our cultural differences make this impossible. Even a fluent Italian speaker would need to have long years of immersion in Italian life to be able to feel something like an Italian's reaction to them. The best that can be achieved is an accurate translation.

The form of the translated work is also important. Clearly if a poem is written in a strict rhythmic and rhyme scheme a perfect translation must follow the same pattern – there are some startlingly good examples of such translations by poets. Cattafi's poems do not rhyme, nor do they have strict rhythm. The fact that almost every line ends in a vowel (and maybe all the exceptions are foreign words) is probably a comment on the Italian language rather than on Cattafi's poetic style. I have tried to make the English versions "sing" as nearly as possible like the originals:

> *Domani apriremo l'arancia*
> *il mondo arancia nel verde domani,*
> *si poserà la nuvola lontana*
> *con le zampe guardinghe di colomba...*   *"Domani"*

> Tomorrow we shall open the orange,
> the world-orange in a green tomorrow.
> The distant cloud will alight
> with wary feet like dove...   "Tomorrow"

The scansion is not identical, since Italian has far more unstressed syllables than English, but the number of stresses in each line has been maintained.

Sometimes the form cannot be matched even to this extent:

> *Ne intendo i segni, i cippi calcinati del confine,*
> *l'ala del fossile confitta sulla costa*
> *le mani rattrappite dei compagni*
> *naufraghi morti nel golfo senza mare.*   *"Antracite"*

> I understand the signs, the calcined stones of the boundary,
> the fossil wing fastened to its side

>   the shrunken hands of wrecked shipmates
>   dead in the oceanless gulf.   "Anthracite"

The second and fourth lines here are very different, but it seemed better (especially given the very variable Italian line form) to aim at the meaning and force of the original images in an equally variable English line form.

For a period Cattafi eschewed the use of punctuation and capitals ("The Tree" and later poems); I have followed him in this respect.

The satisfaction derived from the activity of translation is two-fold. There is the continual challenge of seeking the "right" or "best" version of a poem, that is, the one which conveys best the meaning and feeling of the original. This process brings a much greater understanding of the poem than would come from reading the original or someone else's translation. It is also undeniable that the activity brings the poet far closer to the translator's heart and mind than is possible from mere reading of poems. However different the character of an English businessman is from an Italian poet, during the process of translating Cattafi's works I have felt at times very close to him – a most rewarding experience.

A contemporary critic and fellow-poet, Sergio Pautasso, wrote that "...Cattafi's poetry is often interwoven with autobiographic and diary-like motifs... But their importance... is not so much in the suggestive description of geographic places of this wonderful itinerary... but rather in the aspect that these places take the moment the poet sets his notes and impressions down on the page. In this precise instant he conveys to us the bare image of a simple annotation in a fantastic world, where everything is in flux and assumes unforeseen aspects and colours..."

Certainly the motif of travel and seafaring feature very largely. His travels through much of Europe are recorded in a series of poems from the early '50s – "Liffey River" and "Prince's Street" represent these in this collection. "On the High Seas" is from the same period:

>   Then problems and dangers disappeared,
>   we saw things in the clear
>   atmosphere, precise, enumerated, in file
>   along the lines which from the window
>   stretch as far as the horizon.
>   ...
>   But ships are noisy in the wind

and rustle in the plane trees in the blankets in the court
                                                    yards,
ships that bring us back to the open
sea from where we came, where
a hand's-breadth of blue costs a great deal
and everything is uncertain, even the azure.

The first extract illustrates Cattafi's continual search for something firm to rely on in life (see also "Something Precise"), but the end is pessimistic as ever – everything remains uncertain.

The war features in a number of poems, but does not seem to have been a major formative experience for the poet. "The Autumn Campaign" uses the theme but without any particular relevance to the experience, and "In the Shetlands" makes no reference to his having been a prisoner there. His Sicilian roots come out in this connection in one poem where he comments that an Italian general addressed the troops as "You Sicilians and we Italians", and there are other cynical comments which make it clear that he was not a fervent fighter for his country.

Cattafi was of course a Catholic, and his religion appears from time to time, mainly in the poems of the '70s. It is perhaps revealing that it does not feature in "One 30th August" written on the second anniversary of his mother's death in 1960. This is one of very few poems that relate to his family and emotional life. He did write the occasional love poem in his youth, but chose to omit these from his own selection of works he wished to be preserved, and there is "To Vittorio", with whom he obviously had a great friendship. Perhaps the greatest exception, however, is "A Sense of Rightness", which surely must have been written to his wife.

In later life Cattafi was clearly very interested in food, and poems like "Winter Figs", "Snails" and "Olives" put the food concerned very much in the forefront – they are there for their own sake, not as symbols. In "On the Feast of the Patron Saint" he amusingly puts the enjoyment of food ahead of religious observance.

A quotation from another critic and poet, Giuseppe Zagarrio, in 1962 summarises the impact of Cattafi's work: "With Cattafi... we are at a level where the two categories of "escape" and "irony" combine in a complex whole. In fact, by "cosmopolitan", in reference to Cattafi, we do not mean a human adventure as a tourist, merely wishful and transitory, or as an empiric-intellectualistic kind of experience, but as an escape from a reality which, precisely through that escape, reveals itself in its exact truth, however hard and painful it might be. The Pirandello-like game of being and seeming lies, obviously, at the sentimental-rational source of Cattafi. But what lends validity to this "game" in Cattafi's adventurous history is the discovery of the "sea", a discovery both naturalistic and psychological... in which the experimentalist will of man on the one hand, and on the other his ethical truth, his moral quest for the message, fit together."

Let Cattafi have the last word, written a few months before his death:

> I have nothing more to tell you
> I have told everything
> that I had to about seas mountains forests
> tribes friendly-hostile...
> driven by necessity
> to a truth clothed in falsehood.

Brian Cole

Spenser is known as the poet's poet. T. S. Eliot suggested that poetry was a mug's game – which would make Spenser the mug's mug. This title, I think, might more properly refer to the translator of verse from one language into the verse of another. And the mugs of all mugs would be those who translate poets contemporary with themselves, or, even, those recently dead. For a start, the material rewards are usually quite small.

The fact is that the translator – or mugger – of well-established dead poets has certain compensations that the translator of contemporaries foregoes. Translators of poets like Homer, Dante, Villon, Camoëns, Goethe, have, first, the work of previous scholars to aid them in preparing versions – though some avoid this support for fear of being influenced in quirky interpretative directions. Second, there are usually previous translations extant that may act as signposts, warning lights or buoys marking wrecks and these may offer some sort of guidance. These two things suggest to the translator at least two possible levels of success: bilinguists may judge the new versions in relation to their proximity to the original; monoglots may consider them in relation to their qualities in comparison with earlier translations – not a negligible compensation. Such translators have two other advantages, though perhaps to greater or lesser extent according to talent and temperament. Most of the poets of the European tradition at least worked within recognisable prosodic systems. Some translators find this a bind, others a challenge, but in any case, attempting some sort of prosodic equivalence provides those translators who are not naturally poets with a more or less external benchmark to measure their progress towards an acceptable version. Again according to talent and temperament, in translating the well and truly dead, the translator avoids all chance of intervention from source authors with a smattering of the target language. You wouldn't want the risk of having to argue with, say, Dante, though it might have been fun of a sort with a soberish Villon and certainly with Laforgue. With certain living sources one might be tempted to suggest that they are famous enough to join the well attested dead.

Lastly, in translating the critically acclaimed dead, whatever else translators trust in it is not in their own unaided critical judgement of the literary value of their source.

By contrast, anyone translating contemporaries, or the recent dead, has a trickier task. For example, in translating Bartolo Cattafi, Brian Cole lacks many of the supports mentioned above. In the area of scholarly support Cattafi is virtually unheard of in Britain, so there is little critical debate or scholarly work in the target language to support the endeavour, and, as Cattafi is a recent contemporary, probably nothing over extensive, exegetical, or readily accessible in Italian. Second, so far as I know, there are very few English-language versions to be used as signposts or warning lights. The translation, then, faces the full power of the judgement of bilinguists with no chance of its being considered the best version when there are no extensive comparisons to be made.

In addition, Cattafi writes a form of free verse so there is no benchmark in established prosodies to give firm support to the translator. This is an intractable problem. The amount of undistinguished free verse which is currently being produced by would-be bards in English – I refrain from speaking of Italian – suggests that even self-proclaimed poets may often have a fairly shaky ear when it comes to this type of verse. The translator, however, has to have a finely tuned ear for free-verse rhythms in *two* languages. This appears to be a tall order. Brain Cole shows in his introduction his awareness of this problem.

At least two other problems face translators of twentieth-century poets. In more or less a European context there have been a couple of tendencies in verse that complicate the task. One is a movement away from the poetic towards contemporary colloquial diction, even dialect. (Cattafi was a Sicilian.) This is an area of language that dictionaries, slow on the uptake anyway, are not very acute at capturing with exactitude of tone and usage. Furthermore, Laforgue elaborated the technique, frequently followed this century, of including in verse technical, scientific and trade jargon, an often abstruse and ephemeral area, equally patchy and transient in dictionaries. Another tendency has been towards the obscure, not to say obscurantist, and difficult in modern verse – for which Pound and Eliot have carried the largest can. But there are also many levels of obscurity caused by buried and glancing personal details and local reference, perhaps encouraged by the dogma of impersonality. Cattafi has been labelled in some senses a "hermetic" poet.

Perhaps an example from a famous twentieth-century poet might illustrate some of the difficulties a translator of near contemporaries might face.

In Eliot's "East Coker" occur these lines:

> In the middle, not only in the middle of the way
> But all the way, in a dark wood, in a bramble,
> On the edge of a grimpen, where is no secure foothold…
>
> ll. 89-91

16

An Italian translator of Eliot, presumably after the end of the 1939-45 War, would have little difficulty in matching up the references to the opening of Dante's *Inferno*. Again the unusual rather archaic sequence "where is no secure foothold" would trigger some caution and inquiry as to allusiveness or rhythmic necessity. But he would be stuck at "grimpen". A reasonably informed guess might suggest something boggish or craggy but why such an obscure word? As Helen Gardner pointed out in *The Composition of Four Quartets*, 1978, it isn't until *The Supplement to the Oxford English Dictionary*, *A-G*, 1972, that the word is recorded – and as of obscure etymology. My *Collins*, as late as 1979, thirteen years after Eliot's death and a generation after his famous usage, does not record it as a word. Eliot's usage is the only recorded lower-case example. "Grim-pen", indeed for translators. It is of course from *The Hound of the Baskervilles* by Conan Doyle. But suppose the unlikely event that our putative nineteen-forties Italian translator was also a Sherlock Holmes buff, read the story in the original English, and remembered this particular word when it occurred in Eliot. This would only be a trigger to more problems. First, should the Italian translation retain the English nonce-word? It doesn't sound very Italian. Should an obscure Italian word for a boggy area, supposing one is available, be found, possibly out of a well known Italian author of, ideally, detective fiction? But the issue is even more complex. Did Eliot, at that point, realize what he was doing or had done? In other words was the Conan Doyle reference intended? If not, a standard Italian word might cover the case. Next, if Eliot *did* intend this reference, was it perhaps a mistake in judgement so close in proximity to the Dante allusion? An Italian might think so and, being an enthusiast for his source author, might, perhaps, be tempted to ignore or conceal the reference. Lastly, if the reference is, indeed, intentional does it carry a kind of irony or purposeful bathos with it? And that is just one word-crux and by no means the most difficult or obscure one that our Italian might find, though with Eliot he would, of course, have the advantage with the allusions to Dante when compared to a translator into German.

All such problems are exacerbated in the translation of less famous close contemporaries and these Brian Cole faces, to greater or lesser degree, in making versions of Cattafi.

But perhaps the greatest difficulty is in the area of finding a free-verse equivalent to the Italian poet – for free-verse rhythm demands an almost perfect ear for the language. Help is hard to get here for convincing rhythms are not generally made by two good ears on separate heads.

Italian, I sometimes think, is closer to English habituations of expression in its idiomatic short-cuts and figurativeness than even French – which sometimes seems in its mix of finicking, contraction and pervasive irony a more distant relative. But both of these languages in their day-to-day usage are very different from English in their rhythms. The case might be illustrated by a line or two of Shakespeare, either:

> Absent thee from felicity awhile
> > And in this harsh world draw thy breath in pain,
> > To tell my story...
> > > > > *Hamlet* V. ii

or:

> > No, this my hand will rather
> > The multitudinous seas incarnadine,
> > Making the green one red.
> > > > > *Macbeth* II. ii

The words "absent", "felicity", "multitudinous" and "incarnadine", are all Latin in origin and fluent in rhythm as opposed to the common English vocabulary of the second line quoted from *Hamlet*, ten syllables, ten words. Shakespeare is aware of the unusualness of the Latinate words in the second line quoted from *Macbeth*; so much so that he almost "translates" in the third. English has both the Latinate and the Anglo-Saxon strain of vocabulary, then, but the crucial difference is that the commonest spoken English centres on the monosyllabic Saxon strand; the learned spectrum derives from Latin and Greek polysyllabic sources. "Alimentation" in French, for example, is a common enough word and seldom best translated as "alimentation". This sort of lack of rhythmic match that Brian Cole faces with free-verse from Italian is illustrated by the differences, say, between "una pietra"/ "one stone", (see *Distanza* p74) to speak roughly, a dactyl and trochee, as opposed to the English, a spondee. One could fiddle about with "single" and "pebble" and so forth but the force and colloquial directness would suffer. The sound of the whole line is enough to set one back even though it is a common enough form of expression:

tra una pie*tra* e l'al*tra* / between one stone and the other

I've italicised the echoes.

When a line is a double trochee as is the next, "due sponde",

18

the direct spoken English equivalent is, oddly enough, a spondee: "two banks". Routinely, Italian lines end on vowels and falling rhythms whereas English lines usually end with consonants and stress, at least in traditional prosody which has tuned our ears for so long.

The matching has to be more subtle than this. Every language has its own sound system and barely a mix or match between them. English, for example, associates initial "gl" frequently with light: glare, gleam, glimmer, glint, glisten, glister, glitter, (gloaming?), gloss, glow. Various spellings of the "er" sound associate with rotation, single or frequentative: (quern?), squirm, twirl, stir, circle, churn, turn – to give a few examples. It is at levels like these that the transposing of free verse should occur, and when it occurs it should not interfere with an equivalent naturalness of phrasing.

The foregoing is intended to give some indication to non-Italian speakers of the difficulties that Brian Cole has faced in giving Cattafi the chance of an English hearing. The Italian poet's own lines may be misappropriated to sum up the translator's, as well as the poet's, perennial predicament. Translators are

> "driven by necessity
> to a truth clothed in falsehood."

Driven is the right word, for despite all I have said above, perhaps the chief requisite among a translator's skills must be an obsession with the source author's work. The finished translation must also have the clout of real poems if that is what they were in the original. It takes years to separate that wheat from that chaff. The poor translator of contemporaries, like Shaw's St Joan, in self-defence can only mutter: with whose judgement may I judge but my own. Brian Cole has made his case: non-Italian speakers will have to trust him until some other obsessive presents further evidence in the shape of new versions.

I can't give readers of Cattafi in English much of a reference point to start from. In his attention to what might be called the mystery of the ordinary, he frequently reminds me of the French poet Follain – which isn't much help – and the short lyrics of the Greek poet Yannis Ritsos which I know only in translation.

Peter Dale

ANTHRACITE

ANTRACITE

COL SOLE DISCESO

Col sole disceso
il mare sommesso
appena arriva
a toccare
la riva

La terra è un fiato
di fumo azzurrino
da dove escono le rondini ebbre
con l'ali indietro
e cadono

S'INALBA

S'inalba il vacuo mondo,
si schiude inerte la mano,
sfuggente il monotono ronzare
della mosca,
        un suono
di tedio nella luce bianca

L'INVERNO SI FA FUMOSO

L'inverno si fa fumoso nella stanza,
attizza lacrime, resine stridenti.

(L'inverno passato
succiato nella pipa dolce
assieme al tuo odore,
rame ricche di fiamme nella veglia,
la festa di noi due
col caldo rosso in mezzo alle gambe,
a cavalcioni, col nostro vino a fianco.)

Crolla un tizzone,
la lanterna del sonno è sempre quieta.

SUNK WITH THE SUN

Sunk with the sun
the submissive sea
scarcely manages
to touch
the shore

The earth is a breath
of clear blue smoke
from which emerge the drunken swallows
with wings swept back
and they fall

THE EMPTY WORLD

The empty world grows white,
the hand opens lifeless,
fleeing the monotonous buzzing
of the fly,
                    a sound
of tedium in the white light

WINTER GROWS SMOKY

Winter grows smoky in the room,
it excites tears, harsh resins.

(Last winter
sucking at the sweet pipe
together with your fragrance,
branches rich with flames in the evening,
the festival of us two
with warm red between our legs,
astride, with our wine by our side.)

A burning coal collapses,
the lantern of sleep is still unlit.

DOMANI

Domani apriremo l'arancia
il mondo arancia nel verde domani,
si poserà la nuvola lontana
con le zampe guardinghe di colomba
sopra il tetto di tegole vecchie
sopra il tempo piovuto rugginoso,
serberò al tuo petto quell'odore
d'arancia viva, di verde domani.

NELL'ATRIO, IN ATTESA

Rimangono in un mucchio scolorito
rose e urine nell'atrio. Ignoto è il regno,
alba e attesa, crepuscolo di nubi dove Dio
s'annida, come un colombo gutturale.
Oscuro è il regno, ospite nell'atrio
mano incerta e straniera stacca al vento
la lampada incostante, scendila al petto
per leggerci l'epigrafe, sugli occhi
se le statue biancheggiano, se un triste
insetto stria la nostra mente.
L'arpa celeste insiste nelle stanze
tra un biondo cerchio di scheletri e di sedie;
arpa che ancora insisti, uccello
della morte lenta, sul fuoco polveroso.

TOMORROW

Tomorrow we shall open the orange,
the world-orange in a green tomorrow.
The distant cloud will alight
with wary feet like doves'
on the roof of ancient tiles
on time turned by rain to rust.
I shall find at your breast that fragrance
of living orange, green tomorrow.

IN THE HALLWAY, WAITING

They live in a discoloured heap
roses and urine in the hallway. Unknown is the kingdom,
dawn and expectation, a dusk of clouds where God
nests, like a guttural pigeon.
Obscure is the kingdom, a guest in the hallway
an uncertain and foreign hand removes from the wind
the unsteady lamp, lowers it to his chest
to read there the inscription, on the eyes
if the statues grow white, if a sad
insect streaks our mind.
The celestial harp persists in the rooms
among a blond circle of skeletons and chairs;
a harp which still persists, a bird
of slow death, on the dusty fire.

DAL CUORE DELLA NAVE

Così è il sole divelto dallo zenit
corpo stanco in viaggio alla deriva
come la rosea memoria già lontana.
Puoi cogliere dal cuore della nave
alga e antracite, i fiori dell'abisso
gli occhi verdi del prato e del mare,
e qui in petto ho una macchia a sinistra
come di nafta che non lascia il golfo,
in più i simmetrici polmoni, ancora ansiosi e sudati,
quasi due gigli estivi.
Il nostro sangue nel gracile topo
come vibra impazzito, come un intimo uccello
un pensiero irreale
quando il cielo s'approssima e al battello
le campane s'inclinano nel freddo.

LIFFEY RIVER

La Birra Guinness ha molte porte scure
sui docks e qualche lume
sparso in un lento
regno di chiatte e di vagoni,
di ruggini vagante lungo il fiume,
dove il cigno e il gabbiano sono amici
col petto bianco puntato contro il fango.
Più avanti, a lato della foce,
un prato di trifoglio nella pioggia:
in mezzo vi s'ammucchiano le nostre
giacche, le anime e i loro
segreti scoloriti, le belle
bottiglie tracannate
da una gola tenera, feroce.
E Cristo passa,
astro avvolto di nebbia o nido
per le stanche farfalle che partono da noi,
dolce luce d'olio.

FROM THE HEART OF THE SHIP

So is the sun uprooted from the zenith
a tired body travelling adrift
like the rosy memory already distant.
You can gather from the heart of the ship
seaweed and anthracite, the flowers of the abyss
the green eyes of the meadow and the sea,
and here on my breast I have a mark on the left side
like oil that will not leave the bay,
in addition the symmetrical lungs, still anxious and sweaty,
like two summer lilies.
Our blood in the delicate rat
how insanely it pulses, like a pet bird
an unreal thought
when the sky comes close and the bells
bend down to the boat in the cold.

RIVER LIFFEY

Guinness Beer has many gloomy gates
to its docks and some light
strewn over a sluggish
kingdom of barges and wagons,
of rust wandering along the river,
where the swan and the seagull are friends
with white breasts levelled against the mud.
Further on, at the side of the estuary,
a meadow of shamrock in the rain;
in the middle our jackets
bunched up like our spirits and their
faded secrets, the beautiful
bottles gulped down
by a delicate throat, so fierce.
And Christ passes by,
a star enveloped in mist or a nest
for the tired butterflies that depart from us,
gentle light of oil lamps.

PRINCE'S STREET

Le grandi ombre sospese nella nebbia
toccano il suolo, vanno
nell'erica degli alti territori,
i Re a cavallo
con fiaccole di fosforo,
i Maghi, gli Emblemi, i Cavalieri.
Non ho l'unguento da mettere sui margini
né la statua che colmi questa nicchia
quando il falco ha fatto il suo viaggio
dal pugno a un cuore.
Copriti il buio del petto, il vuoto sibilante
se il vento entra in Prince's Street come
in un lungo sentiero illuminato.
Nella tasca del nero
impermeabile che sventola al mio fianco
c'è il fiammifero spento, c'è il leggero
tabacco che fumano i fantasmi.

PRINCE'S STREET

The great shadows hanging in the mist
touch the ground, walk
in the heather of the highlands,
the Kings on horseback
with torches of phosphorous,
the Counsellors, the Regalia, the Knights.
I do not have the unguent to put on the edges
nor the statue to fill this niche
when the hawk has made his journey
from the fist to a heart.
Cover the darkness of your breast, the sibilant emptiness
if the wind comes into Prince's Street
as into a long lighted footpath.
In the pocket of the black
raincoat which flaps at my side
there is the spent match, there is the light
tobacco that is smoked by ghosts.

PARTENZA DA GREENWICH

Si parte sempre da Greenwich
dallo zero segnato in ogni carta e in questo
grigio sereno colore d'Inghilterra.
Armi e bagagli, belle
speranze a prua,
sprezzando le tavole dei numeri
i calcoli che scattano scorrevoli
come toppe addolcite
da un olio armonioso, in un'esatta
prigione.
Troppe prede s'aggirano tra i fuochi
delle Isole, e navi al largo,
piene, panciute, buone
per essere abbordate dalla ciurma
sciamata ai Tropici
votata alla cattura
di sogni difficili, feroci.
Ed alghe, spume,
il fondo azzurro in cui
pesca il gabbiano del ricordo
posati accanto al grigio
disteso colore
degli occhi, del cuore, della mente,
guano australe ai semi
superstiti del mondo.

DEPARTURE FROM GREENWICH

You always depart from Greenwich
from the zero marked on every map and on this
calm grey, the colour of England.
Bag and baggage, high
hopes on the prow,
scorning the table of numbers
the computations that spring up flowing
like sweetened patches
from a harmonious oil, in a correct
prison.
Too much prey roves across the fires
of the Island, and ships on the high seas,
full, big-bellied, fit
to be boarded by the crew
that swarmed to the Tropics
devoted to the capture
of dreams difficult and fierce.
And seaweed, foam,
the blue depths in which
fishes the seagull of memory,
set beside the expanse
of grey, the colour
of the eyes, of the heart, of the mind,
southern guano for the surviving
seeds of the world.

ANTRACITE

Fabbriche e treni perdono lucore,
invecchiano, sbiadiscono col tempo,
sconfinano nel bigio della nebbia.
L'antracite perdura, abbasso, nera,
fragile, dura, riflessi di metallo,
terra chiusa e remota
a lumi spenti.
Ne intendo i segni, i cippi calcinati del confine,
l'ala del fossile confitta sulla costa
le mani rattrappite dei compagni
naufraghi morti nel golfo senza mare.
Può darsi avvenga domani un altro rogo
non l'aperta l'allegra combustione
che macchia l'aria di fumo e d'amaranto,
la soffocante perdita dell'anima
noi incastrati nell'ombra.

Penso alla pioggia, alla cenere, al silenzio
che l'uragano lascia amalgamati
nella vergine lapide di melma
dove drappelli d'uomini e di bestie
verranno ancora a imprimere
un transito nel mondo,
all'alba ignari sul nero
cuore del mondo.

ANTHRACITE

Factories and trains lose their splendour,
they grow old, they fade with time,
they trespass on the grey of the fog.
Anthracite lasts, down there, black,
brittle, hard, reflections of metal,
earth closed and remote
with lights extinguished.
I understand the signs, the calcined stones of the boundary,
the fossil wing fastened to its side
the shrunken hands of wrecked shipmates
dead in the oceanless gulf.
It may be that tomorrow another funeral pyre will rise
not the open joyous combustion
that stains the air with smoke and amaranth,
the suffocating loss of the soul
ourselves embedded in the darkness.

I think of the rain, of the ashes, of the silence
which the hurricane leaves behind, mixed
in the virgin slab of mud
where troops of men and beasts
will again come to engrave
their passage through the world,
unaware at dawn on the black
heart of the world.

IL GIORNO DOPO

L'autunno ha mari teneri, ha colori
che calme navi tagliano; cadranno
foglie e cieli sospesi per un filo.
Andare sino all'albero, sedersi,
entrare in confidenza con l'inizio
di radiche più avide e vive verso il basso.
Abbiamo accanto povere fredde cose,
bucce, bottiglie, frammenti di memoria,
più in là c'è il mare.
"L'ultima domenica", e ci trovi
ancora ansanti, il cuore
un poco stanco per la festa,
branco che più non fugge, prede
colorite dal ferro irto nel mondo
dal vino, dai fuochi solitari.
Ci vinse
questa striscia di fumo sulla terra,
fu sempre obliqua l'ombra
che ci seguì in silenzio.

THE DAY AFTER

Autumn has gentle seas, it has colours
which still ships cut through; leaves
will fall and skies suspended by a thread.
To walk as far as the tree, to sit down,
to enter into intimacy with the beginning
of roots more eager and lively towards their tips.
We have nearby poor cold things,
fruit peelings, bottles, fragments of memories,
further on is the sea.
"The last Sunday", and here you find
still out of breath, the heart
a little tired by the feast,
a crowd that flees no more, victims
coloured by the bristling steel of the world
by wine, by solitary fires.
Here arrived
this streak of smoke on the earth,
it was always crooked, the shadow
which followed us in silence.

ARCIPELAGHI

Maggio, di primo mattino
la mente gira su se stessa come
un bel prisma un bel cristallo un poco
stordito dalla luce.
Dal soffitto si stacca
neroiridato ilare il festone
delle mosche,
posa su grandi carte azzurre
riparte e lascia
ronzando isole minime, arcipelaghi
forse d'Africa e d'Asia.
Intanto in cielo sempre più si svolge
la mesta bandiera della luce.
Prima di sera l'unghia
scrosta l'isole
le immagini superflue.
Le carte ridiventano deserte.

SOTTOZERO

A novembre andammo sottozero.
                              Il fiume
aveva foglie gialle di platani e colori
su cui l'occhio patisce: acciaio, bitume,
quello della biscia
che scorre lungo i sogni velenosi.
Nella cabina da tempo sommersa (primo
piano d'albergo, rue de Tours)
indossammo la maglia più pesante,
mangiata dalle tarme.
L'unico modo per fingerci vivi
era colpire il cuore: poi tirare
l'ossidata maniglia dell'allarme.

ARCHIPELAGOS

May, in early morning
the mind turns on its very self like
a fine prism a fine crystal a little
bewildered by the light.
From the ceiling detaches itself
the iridiscent black merry festoon
of the flies,
it comes to rest on great blue maps
departs and leaves,
buzzing, small islands, archipelagos
perhaps of Africa and Asia.
Meanwhile in the sky is ever more displayed
the mournful banner of the light.
Before evening the claw
peels off from the island
superfluous images.
The maps become deserts again.

BELOW ZERO

In November we went below zero.
                                  The river
had yellow leaves of planes and colours
on which the eye suffers: steel, bitumen,
that of the slow worm
which glides along venomous dreams.
In the cabin, flooded for some time (first
floor of the hotel, rue de Tours)
we put on our thickest woollens,
moth-eaten as they were.
The only way to pretend we were alive
was to strike our hearts; then to pull
the rusty handle of the alarm.

IN ALTOMARE

Poi problemi e pericoli scomparvero,
vedemmo nella tersa atmosfera
cose precise, numerate, in fila
lungo le linee che dalla finestra
si tendono fino all'orizzonte.
Muovere acque, rompere molecole,
fendere l'aria furono gesti facili,
passare dal moto alla quiete
e viceversa un gioco.
Pesava in cielo il cerchio del futuro
rinfrescato talvolta dall'odore
celeste dell'ozono
da uno scroscio di pioggia.
Prima d'estate – sirene percorrevano i quartieri –
pensammo a chiare immagini di fuoco.
Non vi furono incendi.
Ma navi rumoreggiano col vento
stormiscono coi platani coi panni dei cortili,
navi che ci riportano nell'alto
mare da dove uscimmo, dove
un palmo d'azzurro costa parecchio
ed è tutto malcerto, anche l'azzurro

QUALCOSA DI PRECISO

Con un forte profilo,
secco, bello, scattante,
qualcosa di preciso
fatto d'acciaio o d'altro
che abbia fredde luci.
E là, sul filo della macchina, l'oltraggio
d'una minima stella rugginosa
che più corrode e corrompe più s'oscura.
Un punto da chiarire, sangue
d'uomo, briciola
vile oppure grumo
perenne, blocco di coraggio.

ON THE HIGH SEAS

Then problems and dangers disappeared,
we saw things in the clear
atmosphere, precise, enumerated, in file
along the lines which from the window
stretch as far as the horizon.
To move waters, to smash molecules,
to rend the air were easy gestures,
to pass from motion to rest
and vice versa was a game.
The circle of the future was heavy in the sky
refreshed sometimes by the celestial
perfume of ozone
from a squall of rain.
Earlier in summer – sirens ran through the quarters –
we thought of clear images of fire.
There were no fires there.
But ships are noisy in the wind
and rustle in the plane trees in the blankets in the courtyards,
ships that bring us back to the open
sea from where we came, where
a hand's-breadth of blue costs a great deal
and everything is uncertain, even the azure.

SOMETHING PRECISE

With a strong profile,
spare, fine, springing,
something precise
made of steel or some other substance
which has cold glints.
And there, on the thread of the machine, the outrage
of a tiny star of rust
which darkens the more it corrodes and corrupts.
A point to be cleared up, blood
of a man, a cheap
crumb or a permanent
clot, a block of courage.

APERTURA D'ALI

E l'apertura d'ali?
Essa varia; ve n'è
di micron, ci centimetri, di metri.
Dipende dal modello, dalla materia, dalla
forza motrice; il motivo, la quota da raggiungere
Ripiegate, richiuse, accantonate
sotto un serto verdissimo, nell'Eden
pasto a tarme felici;
oppure sottoghiaccio coi relitti, ossa
regali, mammut, mosche spente
in fondo all'ambra del tempo.
Camminammo più a lungo che potemmo,
spesso vedemmo, alto nella memoria, doloroso,
un bianco stormo di brandelli... (appena
un gioco, un aiuto, una finzione
se sulla scena del deserto il fuoco
s'apprende alla pelle delle prede
se il gelo aggruma nomi disumani).
Un battito d'ali su per le vaste
pareti della memoria non ci sottrae
all'ombre che ci seguono; la iena,
il lupo, gli angeli
abietti dall'obliquo incedere.

LA PAZIENZA

Dovemmo fare cataloghi
dividere le cose
metterle nel calibro
pesarle.
I conti non tornavano, le cose
sovente cambiavano colore,
consistenza, sapore, dimensione.
A occhio allora scegliemmo,
a fiuto, fidando nell'istinto.
I risultati non furono migliori.
In ogni caso ci volle sofferenza
la pazienza che logora la polpa
perché l'osso risplenda.

WINGSPAN

Is it the opening of wings?
It changes; where there is nothing
of microns, of centimetres, of metres.
It depends on the model, the material,
the motive power; the objective, the height to be reached.
Folded again, closed up, angular
under the greenest of garlands, in Eden
a feast for happy moths;
or else under the ice with wreckage, bones
of kings, mammoths, dead flies
deep in the amber of time.
We walked beyond our strength,
often we saw, deep in memory, grieving,
a flock of white rags... (hardly
a game, a helping hand, a sham
if on the scene of the desert the fire
cleaves to the skin of its prey
if the frost collects dehumanised names).
A beating of wings up to the vast
cliffs of memory does not take us away
from the shadows that pursue us; the hyena,
the wolf, the vile
angels with their falsely majestic gait.

PATIENCE

We had to make catalogues
divide things up
put them in a calibrator
weigh them.
It did not work out, things
often changed colour,
consistency, taste, dimensions.
We then selected by eye,
by flair, trusting our instinct.
The results were not better.
In every case there was a need for suffering
the patience that wears out the flesh
so that the bone shines through.

BAEDEKER

Il faro è visible, vicino,
il mare anche nell'alto
inverno è caldo,
sabbia candida e fine,
                    in questa
stagione non è caro.
E non è vero. In questa
e in ogni altra stagione
se fai parte del quadro
darai un'orribile moneta.
Scivola, vola,
non immergere un dito,
non indagare sulle squame d'indaco.
I vecchi ingranaggi sono pronti
e precisi, prudenti.
Udrai anche cantare.
Scappa, metti
ali ai piedi
tappi di cera agli orecchi.

INIZIO

Ebbe inizio nell'ombra, in un angolo lontano
dai luoghi normalmente frequentati.
Quando la spora attesa, il virus remigando giunse
alla terra promessa, in qualche
approdo del cuore per mettervi le tende.
In tal modo nacquero premesse
di frutti estivi,
fiammeggianti pericoli, calure.
Si richiese l'aiuto d'amuleti,
di formule inutili, d'auguri
finché l'opera pervenne a compimento.
Indi ebbe inizio una nuova attesa.

BAEDEKER

The lighthouse is in sight, nearby,
the sea even in the depths
of winter is warm,
the sand clean and fine,
                              in this
season it is not dear.
And it is not true. In this
and in every other season
if you become part of the picture
you will pay a dreadful price.
Slip away, fly,
do not dip in a finger,
do not delve into the indigo scales.
The old cogs are ready
and precise, cautious.
You will also hear singing.
Flee, put
wings on your feet
plugs of wax in your ears.

BEGINNING

It had its beginning in the shadow, in a corner far
from places normally frequented.
When the long-awaited spore, the roving virus reached
the promised land, in some
landfall of the heart to pitch its tents.
In such a way were born forerunners
of summer fruits,
fiery dangers, stifling heat.
The help of amulets was called for,
of useless formulas, of soothsayers
until the work reached its fulfilment.
Then a new wait had its beginning.

UN 30 AGOSTO

Si vide subito che si metteva bene:
eventi macroscopici nessuno,
il sole ad un passo da settembre
diede la prima razione
alle isole di fronte,
il mare mandò lampi di freschezza,
il caldo soltanto fra tre ore,
un immenso celeste, ancora un giorno
per l'uva e gli altri frutti di stagione,
tra i pochi rumori di paese
l'ossigeno sibilando disse
di non farcela più con quel suo cuore.
Di primo mattino la morte di mia madre.

LA BESTIA

E come fai a sapere a prevedere
che se affondi il braccio
in un'acqua di pretto celeste
scatta su dal nulla
con tumulto di bolle l'immonda
bestia che ti azzanna
e per sempre ti avvince il braccio.
Dolcemente golosa del tuo sangue
dovrai nutrirla nasconderla coprirla
con la manica della giacca.

ONE 30TH AUGUST

It was immediately clear that things were getting better:
no macroscopic events,
the sun one step away from September
gave the first rations
to the islands in front,
the sea sent out flashes of coolness,
the heat only three hours away,
an immensity of blue, another day
for the grapes and the other fruits of the season,
among the quiet sounds of the countryside
the hissing oxygen said
no more could be done with her heart.
Early in the morning the death of my mother.

THE BEAST

And how can you know and foresee
that if you submerge your arm
in a water of pure azure
there springs up from nowhere
with a tumult of bubbles the foul
beast who seizes you in his fangs
and for ever captures your arm.
Gently gorging on your blood
you will have to feed, hide, shelter him
with the sleeve of your jacket.

AQUILE, MOSCHE, LEPIDOTTERI

Seccamente dichiaro
su questo tema assurdo:
non amo gli alati.
Aquile, mosche, lepidotteri
fuori del mio interesse.
Fuori dei piedi.
Senza alzare il tono della voce
ripeto che l'argomento fuoco
falena il basso l'alto
l'ali bianche le nere
le squame le piume le membrane
gli angeli dall'ali dolorose
gli esorcismi del giorno e della notte
ripeto: argomento
da lasciare alla porta.
Un'inutile porta chiusa a chiave
per Loro, inutilmente.
Appunto: fate pure,
parlate di corda, in questa casa
senza nome né numero
la vecchia operazione.

EAGLES, FLIES, LEPIDOPTERA

Bluntly I declare
on this absurd subject:
I do not like winged creatures.
Eagles, flies, lepidoptera
are outside my field of interest.
Out of my way.
Without raising the tone of my voice
I repeat that the focus of the subject
the moth the lowly the lofty
white wings black ones
scales feathers membranes
the angels with the sorrowing wings
exorcisms of the day and of the night
I repeat: a subject
to be left at the door.
A useless door locked tight
against Them, uselessly.
Exactly: do as you please,
speak of strings, in this house
without name or number
the old operation.

METEOROLOGIA

Durevoli tuoni a nord,
narici dilatate per tirare
più ossigeno,
aria di dramma,
occhi lampeggianti,
impermeabile buono per un *quai*
delle nebbie.
Avemmo una partenza nebulosa,
seguì tutta la scala fahrenheit.
Il cuore copia il tempo, emette
bollettini discordi, dolorosi,
cose scritte nel quadro del barometro.
Infine a sorpresa venne fuori
il quanto mi dai
mi devi molto
questi sono pochi.
L'alte e basse, le alterne
pressioni simulate,
messinscena i cumuli ed i nembi:
mai era stata in possesso di meteore,
d'occhi simili al cielo per un lampo
per un palmo pulito di sereno.

DIETRO, DENTRO

Dietro il muro, la siepe, il paravento,
dietro un foglio di carta, dietro un velo
d'elastica coscienza,
dietro pelle ossa tessuti
della tua cassa
toracica, nel centro
quasi, un poco a sinistra,
dentro i quattro scomparti della pompa,
dentro al fetido
buio biologico...

METEOROLOGY

Continuous thunder in the north,
nostrils dilated to draw in
more oxygen,
an air of drama,
eyes flashing,
raincoat good for a *quai*
in the mists.
We had a foggy departure,
it went through the whole Fahrenheit scale.
The heart copies the weather, issues
conflicting bulletins, distressing,
things written in the glass of the barometer.
At last surprisingly it came out
how much you give me
you owe me a lot
these are not much.
The highs and the lows, the alternating
simulated pressures,
a stage set with cumulus and rainclouds:
never had it possessed meteors,
eyes like the sky in a flash of lightning
in a polished span of clear sky.

BEHIND, WITHIN

Behind the wall, the hedge, the screen,
behind a sheet of card, behind a veil
of elastic conscience,
behind skins bones fabrics
of your thoracic
cavity, in the centre
more or less, a little to the left,
inside the four chambers of the pump,
inside the fetid
biological darkness...

A VITTORIO

Mio amico,
                    oggi è il dieci settembre
millenovecentosessantadue
e fa ancora caldo
benché siano le undici di sera.
La città è Milano
la stessa città dove tu vivi.
Seduto a questo tavolo bruciato
dalle cicche, senza più vernice,
bollato dal fondo dei bicchieri,
nella casa che conosci.
Ti scrivo per dirti
che quanto prima me ne vado.
Da uomo a uomo voglio dirti grazie
e chiederti scusa delle cose
che fui costretto a darti
quello che fu possibile cavare,
la farina la crusca
uscite dal mio sacco,
di cui ci sarà presto l'inventario.
Vorrei che tu fermassi nella mente
la mia vera sostanza soprattutto
che dalla tua ebbe
luce, vento, profilo
– ignoro che profitto seppe trarne
la mia greve difficile sostanza.
E rientri nei calcoli la sola
verde foglia velenosa,
forma di lancia
rivolta di più verso il mio petto
(conosci i modi offerti dalla vita
di saggiare la morte, tu, con le tue mani,
di attrarla a te, puntartela sul petto
per insania, viltà verso la vita?).
Tutto fu cotto ad un vero fuoco.
Ed ora
tutto è in un fermo vetro trasparente.
Questa amicizia fu per me qualcosa
che non può con l'altro
connettersi, eguagliarsi
nell'amalgama,

TO VITTORIO

My friend,
                today is the tenth of September
nineteen hundred and sixty two
and it is still warm
although it is eleven o'clock at night.
The city is Milan
the same city where you live.
Sitting at this table burnt
by cigarette ends, with no paint left,
stamped by the bottoms of glasses,
in the house that you know.
I am writing to tell you
that as soon as possible I am going away.
Man to man I want to thank you
and to beg your pardon for the things
that I was compelled to give you
that which it was possible to obtain,
the flour the bran
which came from my bag,
of which there will soon be an inventory.
I would like you to fix in your mind
above all my true substance
which from yours took
light, wind, profile
– I do not know what benefit was drawn by
my burdensome difficult substance.
And let me not overlook the only
poisonous green leaf,
spear-shaped
turned more towards my breast
(you know the ways offered by life
to taste death, you, with your own hands,
to draw it to you, to point it at your breast
through insanity, cowardice in the face of life?).
Everything was cooked on a real fire.
And now
everything is in a hard transparent glass.
This friendship was for me something
that cannot be compared,
equated with anything else
in the combination,

bigia spuma, buon sasso,
sabbia sfuggente,
e tu fosti ineguagliabile qualcuno
alta onda smagliante nel gran mare,
cuore saldo e preciso
illimitato cuore fantasioso.
Questa immagine ho avuto,
questa mi porto chiusa dentro il sacco.
Dovrei dirti di come me la passo,
l'ansia, l'affanno
– buffi gesti del muscolo cardiaco –
l'aria che manca se di poco m'affaccio
al luogo dove andrò.
Comunque ti formulo la mia
speranza-promessa:
appena posso
da una cella celeste o infernale
farti una buona
tenace, terrestre compagnia.
Ti dovevo tanto.   Ti saluto.

grey foam, good stone,
receding sand,
and you were someone without peer
a dazzling high wave in the great sea,
a heart steadfast and precise
a heart of infinite fantasy.
This image I have had,
this I carry shut inside my bag.
I should tell you how I am getting on,
the anxiety, the breathlessness,
– strange actions of the cardiac muscle –
shortage of breath if for a little I present myself
at the place where I shall go.
However I formulate for you my
hope-promise:
as soon as I can
from a celestial or infernal cell
to make you a good
steadfast, earthly companion.
I owed you so much.   Farewell.

ANABASI

Auspici ed auguri s'opposero.
Sulla soglia un piede s'impuntò,
                nel viaggio
avemmo presagi che solo pochi ignorano.
Anabasi e non un'ombra
di rimpianto per i calmi
quartieri, l'estivo
l'invernale.
La mente non capisce questo amore
per certi posti remoti dell'interno,
insidiosi, inospiti,
di barbara bellezza.
Non capisce
la necessaria perdita nei boschi.

TIMONIERE

Quindi andai da lui e gli dissi:
Ti prego accosta a dritta
è quello l'arcipelago del cuore.
Mi guardò e sorrise,
mi diede un colpo sulla spalla,
invertì come un fulmine la rotta
e fuggimmo agli antipodi dell'isole
mettendo nelle vele molto vento.
Aveva al timone mani salde,
occhi acuti per tutto,
isole, scogli, cuori.
Comunque ero caduto in tentazione.
Era questo lo scopo delle isole.

ANABASIS

Predictions and wishes conflicted.
On the threshold a foot stumbled,
                              on the journey
we had omens that only a few did not understand.
Anabasis and not a shadow
of regret for the peaceful
quarters, in summer
in winter.
The mind does not understand this love
for certain places deep in the interior,
insidious, inhospitable,
of barbarous beauty.
It does not understand
the necessary losses in the forests.

HELMSMAN

Therefore I went to him and said:
would you please steer to starboard
that is the archipelago of the heart.
He looked at me and smiled,
he gave me a pat on the shoulder,
changed course like lightning
and we flew to the other side of the island
putting much wind in the sails.
He had at the helm steady hands,
eyes sharp to miss nothing,
islands, reefs, hearts.
But still I had fallen into temptation.
That was the purpose of the island.

LETTERA DALL'ENTROTERRA

Dovrei ora parlarvi dell'estate
in questo posto
vetrocemento
asfalto acciaio
ma l'agosto ha frescure insospettate
luce di mare
tende verdi drizzate sulla costa
qualche uccello sul molo
(benché di molto qui si sia addentro
nella terra
e voi direte che pazze fantasie).
Finito ch'ebbe il fuoco di smussarsi
persi i troppi spigoli taglienti
riconobbi la vera compagnia
ogni cosa che onoro è appesa al muro
non più in giro
mescolata all'altro.
Così si cambia genere di vita
si ricorda l'estate nell'inverno
in una cella spersa nella terra
messinscena col mare
con la memoria.

LETTER FROM THE INTERIOR

I should now talk to you about summer
in this place
vitreous cement
asphalt steel
but August has unsuspected coolnesses
light from the sea
green tents set up on the coast
some bird on the jetty
(although we are a long way
inland
and you will say what insane fantasies).
As soon as the fire ceased to smooth its edges
and the too sharp corners were lost
I recognised the true company
everything that I honour is hung on the wall
no longer circulating
mixed with the other.
Thus the quality of life changes
summer is remembered in winter
in a cell lost inland
a stage setting with the sea
with memory.

LA CAMPAGNA D'AUTUNNO

Li lasci in disparte, non ci pensi
e l'estate è finita,
in questa luce tornano con ali
pesanti, misuri
l'inclinazione dello scafo.
Merce cattiva bilanciata male,
di troppi gradi andato fuor di squadra.
Ombre, caligine, orizzonte
ventoso.
Anche qui folate,
nodi d'aria ancora molto lenti.
Appena a riva il tempo
per qualche sasso, conchiglia, ripartire.
La campagna d'autunno.
Pensa all'acqua all'orribile tempesta
che irrompe nel bicchiere,
al terribile fuoco che tu porti
in tasca, in una busta
di fiammiferi.

LA SCATOLA CINESE

Mi correte addosso
dai quattro angoli
urlando
e disputate a morsi
entro di me
banchettate
miei nemici e compagni.
Anch'io metto le mani
nella scatola cinese,
mangio,
con vertigine guardo
i gradini infiniti della scala.

THE AUTUMN COUNTRYSIDE

You leave them on one side, you do not think of them
and summer is over,
in this light they return with wings
heavy, you measure
the angle of the fuselage.
Shoddy goods badly balanced,
by too many degrees off the track.
Shadows, mists, windy
horizons.
Here too are flurries,
knots of air still very slow.
Scarcely ashore it is time
for some rock, shell, to depart again.
The autumn countryside.
Think of the water, of that dreadful storm
which overflows in the glass,
of the terrible fire that you carry
in your pocket, in a folder
of matches.

THE CHINESE BOX

You run to attack me
from the four quarters
screaming
and you compete for morsels
of my entrails
you feast on
my enemies and my friends.
I too put my hand
into the Chinese box,
I eat,
I am giddy looking at
the numberless rungs of the ladder.

TIRRENO E JONIO

Si cambiano sovente i connotati
diventano violenti
schiumano sul luogo dello scontro
e le seppie schizzano inchiostro
le triglie s'aggirano torve come squali
i passeggeri si tengono alle maniglie
se l'acciuga avanza come un mostro.

POLPETTE

Davanti ad un brandello
di carne spiaccicato sulla carta
mia madre era sempre in bilico
se aggiungere molto pangrattato
o le patate
bollite e schiacciate.
Mi tiravo in disparte
me ne andavo nell'ombra
a rigirarmi in bocca una foglia
del mio albero
il basilico.

NELLA FESTA DELLA SANTA PATRONALE

Ottanta giorni prima di Natale
nella nera pignatta
nell'acqua biancastra
schiuma e sbuffa la testa di maiale
il vino alza la cresta nel boccale
se non bevessi vino
non mangiassi maiale
sarei un'ala
appuntata ai piedi patronali.

THE TYRRHENIAN SEA AND JONIO

They often change their appearance
they become violent
there is froth on the field of play
and the squid squirt ink
the mullet loiter sullenly like sharks
the passengers hold on to the handrails
if the anchovy advances like a monster.

RISSOLES

Before a fragment
of flesh squashed on the paper
my mother was always undecided
whether to add a lot of fried breadcrumbs
or potatoes
boiled and mashed.
I took myself aside
I went off in the shadows
to revolve in my mouth a leaf
from my tree
the basil.

ON THE FEAST OF THE PATRON SAINT

Eighty days before Christmas
in the black cauldron
in the whitish water
the pig's head foams and snorts
the wine raises its crest in the jug
if I did not drink wine
did not eat pork
I would be a wing
pinned to the saintly feet.

SALVIA GINEPRO ROSMARINO

L'isola ha folti ciuffi
di salvia ginepro rosmarino
ramoscelli cedevoli
ai venti di settentrione
vestiti di verdesperanza
e scaglie lische
di pesce isolano
essiccate dal sole sugli scogli.
Si sbaglia chi arrivando a queste coste
crede che dietro alle grandi
essenze d'aroma
si stendano lunghe mense
montagne d'arrosti fumiganti.
Le tre piante pazienti
da secoli profumano l'aria
e aspettano invano
che da un luogo lontano
giunga un bastimento carico di...
Portatrici di favole odorose
miti eredi di caste talee
se posso vi cambio in blocco
con forti articoli animali
milizie giustiziere
vipere scorpioni vedove nere
tutt'insieme scattanti
appena suona il passo di quel piede.

AL NOME DI LOURDES

Perché s'infuriano i manzi nell'arena
al nome di Lourdes
chi si muove chi s'agita furente
sotto la loro pelle?
Conosciamo il Maligno
egli sovente entra ed esce da noi.
Falli fumare stridere schiumare
sferza quel fuoco con la Tua acqua.

SAGE JUNIPER ROSEMARY

The island has thick tufts
of sage juniper rosemary
twigs that yield
to the winds of the North
clothed in hopegreen
and smooth scales
of island fish
dried up by the sun on the rocks.
He is mistaken who arriving on these coasts
believes that behind the great
essences of perfume
long months stretch out
mountains of smoking roasts.
The three patient plants
have for centuries perfumed the air
and they wait in vain
for the arrival from some distant place
of a ship loaded with...
Bearers of odorous fables
myths heir to pure cuttings
if I can I will change you en masse
with strong animal products
armies acting as executioners
vipers scorpions black widows
springing all together
the step of that foot makes scarcely a sound.

AT THE NAME OF LOURDES

Why do bullocks in the arena fly into a rage
at the name of Lourdes
who moves who is furiously stirring
under their skin?
We know the Malign One
he often enters and leaves us.
Make them smoke grate foam
scourge that fire with Your water.

NELLE SHETLAND

Questi li tengo chiusi nel recinto
sull'ultimo scoglio a Nord
che in Europa possiedo
insieme con la Regina dei Britanni.
All'altezza di questo parallelo
le cose cambiano
d'estate la notte non ha spazio
la patata il fungo il pomodoro
la carota la mela la cipolla
vengono per nave dalla Scozia
qui cresce un'erba dura
nana giallastra sulla torba
pastura che fa deformi i ponies
dilata una gran pancia
su gracili gambe
ma la testa è di grande splendore
nobile ben sbalzata intelligente
un ciuffo arruffato sulla fronte
le pecore acquistano un pessimo carattere
ottuse ombrose onuste
di ricchissima lana
i ladri d'aringhe i lesti mendicanti
ad ali aperte gridano sfrontati
gabbiani d'occhio avido
instancabili voci
i pulcinella di mare
si perdono accecati
dietro un lampo d'argento di sott'acqua
la terna artica
disegna l'eleganza su una lastra
immensamente simile alla morte.
Erano questi i segni e le figure
d'una stagione attenta
affettuosa
d'un album uscito a Nord nell'ultima
mia Thule nell'ultima
parte della mia vita.

IN THE SHETLANDS

These I hold locked in the enclosure
on the last rock in the North
which I possess in Europe
together with the Queen of the Britons.
At the level of this parallel
things change
in summer the night does not have room
the potato the mushroom the tomato
the carrot the apple the onion
come by ship from Scotland
here grows a tough grass
dwarf yellowish on the peat
pasture which deforms the ponies
dilates a great belly
on delicate legs
but the head is of great splendour
noble proudly held intelligent
a ruffled forelock on the brow
the sheep acquire a very bad character
obtuse irritable burdened
with very rich wool
the herring thieves the nimble beggars
with open wings cry impudently
seagulls with eager eye
tireless voices
the buffoons of the sea
lose themselves blinded
on a silver flash under the water
the arctic tern
draws elegance on a block of stone
immensely similar to death.
These were the signs and the forms
of a watchful affectionate
season
from an album which came from the North in my Ultima
Thule in the last
part of my life.

I FICHI DELL'INVERNO

I fichi dell'inverno
vengono ai rami stravolti dal freddo.
Chiusi sodi caparbi
dissimili dagli estivi
svenevoli compagni
sono rossi di dentro come un tramonto
gelido senza giallo
selvatici sospettosi
a ogni stormir di fronda
serrano fra le labbra asprigne
una riga di zucchero.
Giunti inaspettati
se ne vanno così
come sono venuti
frammenti erranti
nel vuoto e nel buio
per un attimo colpiti dalla luce

LUMACHE

Lumache e lumache
le più note
sono come levrieri
di carne chiara
collo di cigno
alte eleganti ben portanti
Le altre
piccole tozze scure
meridionali chiuse
d'animo e guscio
di cellule forti
vanno anche all'estero per mezza
foglia di lattuga
diventano velociste
fanno i mille ad ostacoli
con sempre più ostacoli
finché muoiono.

WINTER FIGS

Winter figs
come on branches twisted by the cold.
Closed solid obstinate
different from those of summer
mawkish companions
they are red inside like a sunset
icy with no yellow
wild suspicious
at every rustle of the leaves
they squeeze between the tart lips
a line of sugar.
Unexpectedly arrived
they go away like this
as they came
wandering fragments
in the void and the dark
for an instant struck by the light.

SNAILS

Snails and snails
the best known
are like greyhounds
with clear flesh
neck of a swan
tall elegant with good bearing
The others
small squat dark
Southerners closed
of mind and shell
with hard cells
would even go abroad for half
a lettuce leaf
they become sprinters
they do the mile with obstacles
with ever more obstacles
until they die.

OLIVE

Lustre matrone
piccole novizie con la faccia in ombra
puttanelle appuntite
vi spoglio del vostro
velo di cellulosa
segretissime polpe
trame sottili che dall'avana andate
al nero antracite
amiche con offerte fantasiose
quattro sensi portate
su piste di decollo
olive drupe fiale
d'essenze altamente volatili
olio in lunghezza larghezza spessore
olio carezzevole e concreto
timidi stormi boschivi
funghi frutti fondenti
rose in un soffio raggrinzite
affumicate
spiccioli d'un sole fumicoso
cibarie sparpagliate sopra i rami
ancora aeree
ancora aclorurate
alunne a volte d'un forte
acido oleico felicemente fenico
vene che passano
d'ottobre e novembre in posti caldi
chi nel vetro vi vede
accalcate malconce confuse
con finta salute
sapore di veleno
vorrebbe rifare il cammino
della scala a pioli
riportarvi ai rami
a una plurima sorte
al cielo dei vostri voli.

OLIVES

Glossy matrons
little novices with your faces in shadow
pointed little strumpets
I strip you of your
veil of cellulose
most secret pulps
slender threads that rise from the Havana
to the black anthracite
friendly girls with fanciful offers
you carry four senses
on take-off runways
olives drupes phials
of highly volatile essences
oil in length breadth thickness
oil mellifluous and real
shy wooded crowds
fused fungi fruits
roses shrivelled in a breath
smoked
small change of a steamy sun
victuals scattered on the branches
still aerial
still chlorided
some time alumni of a strong
oleic acid happily carbolic
veins that pass
from October and November in warm places
he who sees you in the jar
crowded battered confused
with feigned health
a taste of venom
would like to retrace the road
of the ladder
back to the branches
to a multiple destiny
to the heaven of your flights.

PORTA

Semplice e umile
discendente da povera pianta
squadrata come Dio volle
resisti loro
rinsaldati in lungo e in largo
in ogni fibra
segnati con vernice fiammeggiante
verranno di notte
urlando ad ali aperte
su di te a valanga
con pugni calci bestemmie
avranno teste d'ariete
puzza di zolfo.

RICONOSCIMENTO

Verso le dodici d'oggi
venticinque settembre settantuno
sulla spiaggia chiamata Marchesana
nel golfo tra i due capi
di Tyndaris e di Milae
trovo – bianca bombata
doppiamente bordata di marrone
d'ottima fattura siciliana –
una conchiglia che fu mia piastra
di riconoscimento
la prima volta
quando andavo per mare combattendo
aspettando la nebbia della morte
ed ora chi si ricorda di che tipo
fosse la mia anima
se cartaginese o romana.

DOOR

Simple and humble
descendant of a poor plant
squared as God wished
resist them
strengthen yourself in height and breadth
in every fibre
mark yourself with fiery paint
they will come by night
howling with open wings
on you like an avalanche
with fists kicks imprecations
they will have heads of rams
the stench of sulphur.

IDENTITY

Towards twelve o'clock today
the twenty-fifth of September seventy-one
on the beach called Marchesana
on the gulf between the two capes
of Tyndaris and Milae
I find – white convex
with a double border of chestnut
of the best Sicilian manufacture –
a shell which was my
identity disc
the first time
I went to sea in battle
waiting for the mist of death
and now who remembers of what type
my soul might have been
whether Carthaginian or Roman.

VISITA

Esitò sul filo della soglia
entrò e fece il giro della stanza
si posò in un angolo d'ombra
benché disvelandosi di poco
si vide ch'era
di struggente bellezza.
Mal me ne incolse quando
un fremito percorse   le sue ali
preda d'un vento interiore
e foglia fiore vagante farfalla
del mio mondo perduto
volò via.

SPACCIO

Spalle petto girello
mi domando perché non debba esserci
una distinta dei prezzi
reni polmone cuore
e un mattatoio
e un pubblico spaccio
di carne umana
docile dolciastra facilmente
assimilabile
divorata da sempre
dietro una trasparenza di metafora.

È QUESTO

Ecco è questo
che butto nella mischia
un cuore ferito
un polso mal collegato con il resto
vorrei riposare in un basso
in un alto rilievo
l'occhio una quieta mandorla di marmo
non muovere un dito.

VISIT

It hesitated on the edge of the threshold
it entered and made a tour of the room
it placed itself in a corner of shadow
although revealing itself only a little
it could be seen that it was
of consuming beauty.
Evil befell me when
a trembling ran through   its wings
prey to some inner draught
and leaf flower wandering butterfly
from my lost world
it flew away.

SALE

Shoulders breast thigh
I wonder why there should not be here
a list of prices
kidneys lights heart
and a slaughter-house
and a public sale
of human flesh
tender sweetish easily
digestible
ever devoured
behind a transparency of metaphor.

HERE IS WHAT

Here is what
I hurl into the fray
a wounded heart
a wrist badly connected with the rest
I should like to relax in a bas relief
in an haut relief
my eye a calm marble almond
not moving a finger.

UN PRATO

Dopo tante stazioni
un prato di trifoglio
di qualsivoglia erba
agibile palestra
pasquale officina
dominicale come un vangelo
gli ulivi d'allora
il Golgota vicino
il guanciale
i tre morti
i cieli assorti nella contemplazione.

UN SENSO GIUSTO

Tutto quello che passa
per le tue mani
ha una dolce impronta
un senso giusto
un sapore di semi
si riscatta dall'onta
del suo essere plumbeo
ogni ruga si spiana
sull'arco della fronte
che da te si diparte
a te ritorna
come un pane sparito
rifiorito nel forno.

DISTANZA

C'è una fredda distanza
lucente e nuda
che non si tenta nemmeno di coprire
nuda irreparabile lucente
tra una pietra e l'altra
due sponde
due invitati nella stessa stanza
che tranquilli la rigirano tra le mani
come i due capi di una lama.

74

A MEADOW

After so many stations
a meadow of clover
of some grass or other
suitable for a training ground
a paschal workshop
dominical as a gospel
the olives of that time
Golgotha nearby
the cushion
the three dead
the heavens rapt in contemplation.

A SENSE OF RIGHTNESS

Everything that passes
through your hands
has a sweet imprint
a sense of rightness
a taste of seeds
redeems itself from the shame
of its leaden existence
every wrinkle is made smooth
on the bow of the brow
which departs from you
returns to you
as a hidden loaf of bread
refreshed in the oven.

DISTANCE

There is a cold distance
shining and naked
which they do not even try to cover
naked irreparable shining
between one stone and the other
two banks
two guests in the same room
who peacefully turn it round between their hands
like the two ends of a sword.

UN LEVRIERO

Come in un arazzo
una scena di giardino
un levriero seduto accanto
a una vasca d'acqua gelata
sullo sfondo le nuvole di marzo
passavano raffiche di frecce
stridevano incruente
nell'aria di cristallo
c'era qualcosa o qualcuno
seduto in un angolo
con le mani incrociate
in posizione di stallo.

SEGNI

Taglia loro la gola
col segno d'un coltello
appèndili in fila a testa in giù
larghi medi sottili
che sgoccioli ben bene
l'inchiostro dei segni
a piè di pagina
nei segni-bacile

UN ALBERO

Ecco un albero scritto bene
in nero in verde e marrone
con le rughe
le foglioline di primavera
gli uccelli sui rami
e gli insetti in processione
i piccoli mostri
che lo venerano in lungo e in largo
e passo passo lo tarlano
ma non d'inverno
quando dormono
nel fitto dell'inchiostro

A GREYHOUND

As in a tapestry
a garden scene
a seated greyhound beside
a pool of frozen water
in the background the march clouds
went by like squalls of arrows
they hissed bloodless
in the crystal air
there was something or someone
sitting in a corner
with hands crossed
in the position of stalemate.

SIGNS

Cut their throats
with the sign of a knife
hang them in a row heads down
the large the medium the thin
so that the ink of the signs
can trickle very easily
at the foot of the page
into the sign-basin

A TREE

Here is a tree writ well
in black in green and brown
with its wrinkles
the little leaves of Spring
the birds on its branches
and the insects in procession
the tiny monsters
which worship every part of it
and step by step they eat into it
but not in winter
when they sleep
in the depths of the ink

PITTURA RUPESTRE

Non sono ancora nato
incubato in caverna dipingo
scene di caccia
di guerra soprattutto
segno fresco e preciso
che viene fuori guizzando da un sangue fresco
segno preciso
come ossa tarso
perone metatarso
pezzi di calcio apparsi già spolpati.

FRATELLI

In fondo alla fossa
non ci sono leoni
non c'è daniele
ma c'è il prossimo tuo
fratellastri e fratelli
mostri verdastri
nella melma del fiele

SIMMENTHAL

Con dolcezza impazzire al declino
di nostra vita
su questa proda di sopravvivenza
attingo al tascapane
                      e posso
dare i nomi più belli al bovino
muscolo rosso cotto nel suo brodo.

ROCK PICTURE

I am not yet born
incubated in a cave I paint
hunting scenes
scenes of war above all
a fresh and precise mark
that comes out quivering from fresh blood
a precise mark
like bones tarsus
fibula metatarsus
pieces of calcium appeared already stripped clean.

BROTHERS

At the bottom of the trench
there are no lions
there is no daniel
but there is your neighbour
half-brothers and brothers
greenish monsters
in the mire of bile

SIMMENTHAL*

Sweetly to go mad on the downslope
of our life
on this shore of survival
I reach into this haversack
           and I can
give the most beautiful names to the cattle
red muscle cooked in its own broth.

*A brand of corned beef.

DURATA

Non c'è carica non c'è
prevedibile durata
c'è la verga di cera ma la fiamma
impinguata di cera impazzisce
nella sala ventosa del re.

PASSERO

Tutti tagliati i tardivi granturchi
bruciati i mucchi di tutte le sterpaglie
estinte e nel ricordo
già stinte le battaglie
la mente mistificante vede
la neve
e sulla neve il passero
malmesso intirizzito tracotante.

GEOGRAFO

Non ho altro da dirvi
ho detto tutto
quel che dovevo su mari monti selve
tribù amiche-nemiche
non ho altro da dirvi
per mentirvi
tutto ho stravolto mutato adattato
a un diverso disegno
ho parlato di me
ho confessato andando
dal massiccio montuoso all'alga all'erba
spinto dalla bisogna
ad una verità vestita di menzogna.

DURATION

There is no set time, no
foreseeable duration
there is the rod of wax but the flame
fattened with wax goes mad
in the windy hall of the king.

SPARROW

The late maize all cut
the piles of all the undergrowth burnt
dead and in the memory
the battle already faded
the mind deceptive sees
the snow
and on the snow the sparrow
shabby freezing strutting.

GEOGRAPHER

I have nothing more to tell you
I have told everything
that I had to about seas mountains forests
tribes friendly-hostile
I have nothing more to tell you
to lie to you
I have upset changed adapted everything
to a different design
I have spoken of myself
I have confessed going
from the mountainous massif to seaweed to grass
driven by necessity
to a truth clothed in falsehood.

PROMESSA

Riscriverò a lungo
minuzioso lento
rientrerò nel folto delle messi
riscoprirò il pruno dentro l'occhio
l'unica cosa che m'interessi.

PROMISE

I shall write again at length
in detail slowly
I shall go back into the thick of the corn
I shall rediscover the thorn in the eye
the only thing that interests me.

BARTOLO CATTAFI was an extremely prolific poet, who published many collections in his lifetime, but, in spite of his popularity in Italy, he has hitherto been almost unknown in the English-speaking world. He was born in Sicily in 1922 and died there in 1979. But he did not spend all his life in Sicily; he was a prisoner of war in the Shetlands and later lived for over twenty years in Milan. During this time he travelled extensively in Europe and Africa. His poems often reflect that restlessness: poems about islands, streets, cities, the sea. Places familiar and unfamiliar to the English reader. Cattafi's travels were not just physical; much of his life was a spiritual quest for meaning in the everyday. Objects such as olives, trees, doors, snails, figs are presented in brief, precise meditations, juxtaposed with unexpected imagery, as he probes the truth behind their concrete existence.

BRIAN COLE recreates these poetic moments in English with great skill, so that we are able to follow Cattafi's search, sharing his urgent feeling of being "driven by necessity" to discover what lies beneath the surface.